数字化教材编委会

主　编　邱　爽　宋雪文

副主编　汪佳瑶　赵冬艳　马金诚

编　者　（以姓氏笔画为序）

马金诚［燕园校友（宁波）投资管理有限公司］

邱　爽（浙江药科职业大学）

汪佳瑶（浙江药科职业大学）

宋雪文（浙江药科职业大学）

张继军（浙江药科职业大学）

赵冬艳（北京中科亿康科技有限公司）

柯　飞（浙江药科职业大学）

PREFACE 前言

随着我国对外交流和国际交往需求日益增长，对跨文化交流人才的需求也与日俱增。为了学习者能更好地适应不同的交际环境，跨文化交流更加顺畅，同时也做好中国优秀传统文化的传播者，我们尝试编写一本立足于实际应用的教材。

本教材注重实际应用能力和综合素养的培养，具有以下特点。

1. 创新教材编写形式，优化英语教学途径。本教材设计为“活页式”，促使学生学用结合。教材共分为七个单元，每个单元分为学习目标、步骤或分类、学生自评、总结反思四大板块，通过明确教学目标、探索启发式问题、完成工作表单、撰写实训体会、优化评价方法等步骤，促使学生养成独立思考习惯、锻炼团队协作能力、总结提升实践经验，逐步具备较强的职业素养。

2. 融入课程思政元素，实现立德树人目标。本教材每个单元都将相关思政元素有机融入工作任务。例如，在市场营销单元的“医药市场调查”部分，培养学生树立重视运用市场调查的意识，培养实事求是和爱岗敬业的职业精神；在商务谈判单元，培养学生树立坚定、正确的价值观、人生观和世界观，在洽谈过程中始终坚守爱国主义精神。同时，本教材通过中西方文化对比，引导学生搜寻和探究文化现象背后的文化内涵，培养探究和弘扬中国文化的优秀品质。

3. 注重理论联系实践，探索知行合一方法。本教材充分考虑专业教学需求，积极发挥校企“双元”育人作用，编者结合多年课堂教学实践及相关企业技能培训工作经验进行编写；特意邀请到北京中科亿康科技有限公司等企业人员，为教学大纲的拟定和内容修订提供了宝贵意见参考。教学项目均为实际案例中筛选出的典型工作任务，切合职业教育特点，做到理论知识深入浅出、难度适宜，实践技能贴近行业需求。

4. 突出医药学科内容，提升职业素养。本教材贴合医药院校学生需求，融合医药院校自身特色，将医药元素融入教材之中，旨在提升学生的医药学科职业素养。其中，市场营销单元引入药品和医疗器械销售方案，商务谈判单元融入药品推广策略和价格谈判，求职面试单元将场景设置为制药和医疗器械企业等，通过诸如此类的情节和场景设计，为学生提供有针对性的实用性案例，有效提高其医药学科职业素养。

本教材主要供高等职业教育本科院校应用英语、外事实务等专业作为跨文化专业课的实训教材使用，也可供有跨文化交流需求的外贸公司、医药企业、翻译公司等作为培训教材使用。

本教材在编写过程中得到了院校领导和老师的大力支持，在此表示衷心感谢！限于时间与水平，教材中难免存在疏漏与不足之处，恳请各界人士批评指正。

编　者

2024 年 2 月

CONTENTS 目录

Unit 1 Business Reception

PPT

Section Ⅰ. Task Steps and Requirements

NO.	Steps	Requirements	Others
1	Before Reception	1. Know about business communication etiquette in various countries. 2. Be able to identify the major differences of invitation letters between China and other cultures. 3. Be able to write formal invitation letters in English.	
2	During Reception	1. Be able to make introductions, exchange business card in an appropriate manner. 2. Be able to use polite expressions in English. 3. Understand the concept of power distance and apply it into practical use. 4. Understand the differences of dining customs between China and UK. 5. Be able to make seating arrangement in Chinese and British way.	
3	After Reception	1. Understand how gift giving varies depending on culture. 2. Be able to give gifts appropriately.	

Section Ⅱ. Task Scenario

You are working in a Chinese pharmaceutical company which is planning a business reception to strengthen its international cooperation. As a receptionist, you are assigned to prepare for the reception. Please finish all the following tasks. You have to take intercultural elements into account.

1. Before Reception

1.1 Terminology and Theories

(1) Which communication method should be adopted to invite your business partner: telephone, fax, written correspondence or others?

(2) What language should be applied in written correspondence?

(3) What is the role of the fixer?

1.2 Writing Invitation Letters

Task 1

What are the common practices in writing invitation letters? Discuss with your partner, decide true(T) or false(F) of the following statements and correct the false one(s).

(1) ________ Use novel and uncommon English words.

(2) ________ Choose words that have only one meaning.

(3) ________ Select words with few or similar alternate meanings.

(4) ________ Use redundant writing style.

(5) ________ Be aware of the alternate spellings in countries that use the same language.

(6) ________ Creating and using new words or slang.

(7) ________ Use a formal tone and correct punctuation to ensure clarity.

(8) ________ Use first name in letter salutations.

(9) ________ Use salutation and closing in your own country's style.

(10) ________ Use compound and compound-complex sentences to make you comprehensible.

(11) ________ Clarify the meaning of words that have more than one meaning.

(12) ________ Use the tone of your own culture to deliver the message adequately.

(13) ________ Use acronyms, emotions and shorthand to compose a letter.

(14) ________ If photocopies to other members of the organization are appropriate, be sure to send them a copy or ask who should receive copies.

(15) ________ "Seven thousand" can be written as "7,000", "7.000" or "7000" in different countries.

Task 2

Discuss within groups: What are the major differences between invitation letters of China and of other cultures?

Task 3

Write an invitation letter based on what you have learned.

2. During Reception

2.1 Terminology and Theories

(1) What are the differences between Person-oriented and Status-oriented verbal styles?

(2) What is power distance according to Hofstede's Five Value Dimensions?

(3) How does a business person from a small power distance country like to be treated?

2.2 Making Introductions

Task

How to address and greet the customers from the following countries? Please fill out the following table.

Countries	Address Forms	Verbal Greetings	Nonverbal Greetings
China			
USA			
UK			
Germany			
Italy			
Brazil			
Egypt			
Iraq			

2. 3 Business Card Exchange

Task 1

Think about the following questions critically:

(1) What information should be included in a business card?

(2) What are the differences between the business card for a domestic customer and for a foreign customer?

(3) Do you know other differences in exchanging business card among different cultures?

Task 2

Please design a business card of your own by filling in the following blank table.

Task 3

Please role play the following scenario based on the instructions and requirements:

Two days before the meeting, you and your manager will pick up one of your customers at the airport. This will be the first time your manager has met the customer.

Instructions and requirements:

(1) It is a group work with 3-4 students.

(2) You need to prepare a 5-10 minutes role play.

(3) Your customer comes from one of the countries in the task of 2.2.

(4) You need to consider proper ways of addressing, greeting and business card exchanging in the scenario.

2.4 Position and Status

People value different things from culture to culture, such as authority, age, education level, profession, etc. To know if you need to acknowledge your client's social status or you just need to be polite in your first meeting is a way to show respect and may leave them with a good impression. Therefore, it's important to know the differences between your culture and your client's.

Task 1

Please look into the different aspects of what your customers value in their country, tick (√) the ones you think are important in deciding a person's position and status in that country.

Cultures	Element(s) that Can Affect One's Social Status						
	Education	Age	Wealth	Occupation	Profession	Taste	Gender
China							
Republic of Korea							
Japan							
Arabian countries							
USA							
Germany							
India							

Task 2

What are the suitable ways to treat your customers from different cultures? Discuss with your partner and fill in the following table. You may take Hofstede's theory of Power Distance into consideration.

Cultures	Ways of Class Distinction
China	
Republic of Korea	
Japan	
Arabian countries	
USA	
Germany	
India	

Task 3

The following table is a summary of the characteristics of High Power Distance and Low Power Distance cultures. Can you give some examples of the two types of cultures respectively?

Characteristics of High and Low Power Distance Cultures		
NO.	High Power Distance	Low Power Distance
1	Minimize social or class inequalities.	Each person has a rightful place in the social order.
2	Question or challenge authority figures.	Actions of authorities should not be challenged or questioned.
3	Reduce hierarchical organizational structures.	Hierarchy and inequality are appropriate and beneficial.
4	Use power only for legitimate purposes.	People with social status have a right to use their power for whatever purposes.

Task 4

Based on the information displayed in the table above, decide which power distance culture the following countries belong to.

Countries	High Power Distance	Low Power Distance
China		
Republic of Korea		
Japan		
Arabian countries		
USA		
Germany		
India		

2.5 Dining Practices

Task 1

What will you say or behave in the following situations?

Situation 1:

You have prepared a splendid dinner to treat your American clients, what will you say to start it?

Situation 2:

A Chinese host/hostess normally prefers to persuade guests to eat more food to show our hospitality. What will you think and respond when your American client say "I'm full"?

Situation 3:

You have just had an excellent dinner in your Greek colleague's home, and it's time for your leaving. You intend to express your gratitude.

Task 2

You are going to set the table for a business dinner to treat your clients from UK. How will you arrange the sequence of table seating in Chinese and British ways respectively? Arrange The Host, The Hostess, The Most Important Female Guest, The Most Important Male Guest, Next Most Important Female Guest and Next Most Important Male Guest in the right seats by filling out the following bold rectangles.

Chinese Way:

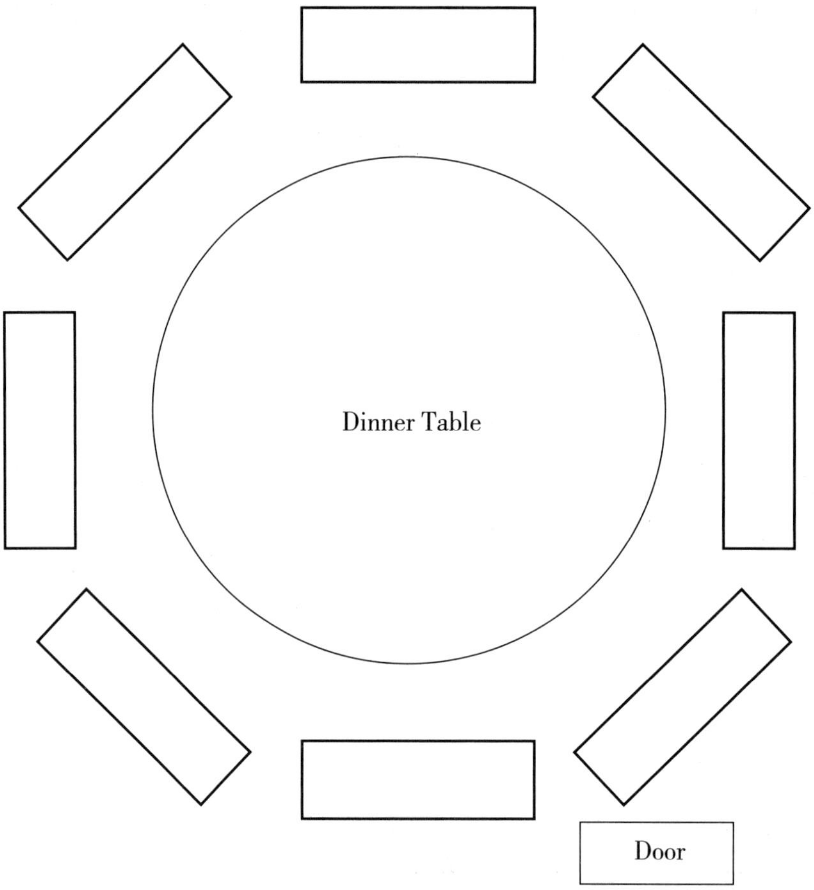

British Way:

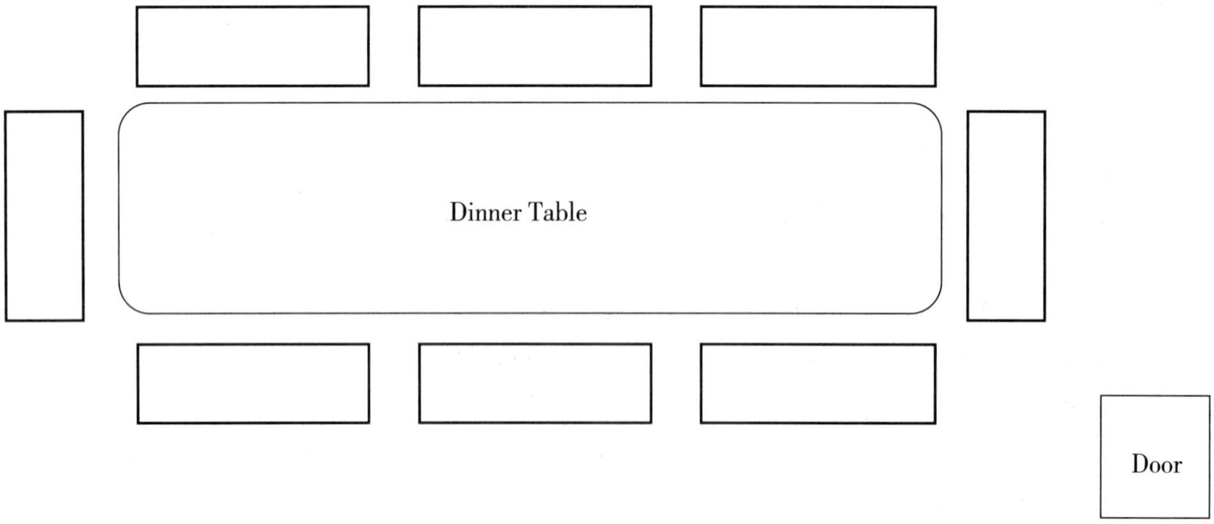

3. After Reception

3.1 Gift Giving

The practice of gift-giving can establish and maintain harmonious business relationship between you and your clients. However, sending an unsuitable gift or giving a gift improperly may cause ill-effects. Therefore, gift-giving calls for one's sensitiveness to personal and cultural differences.

Task 1

Can you list some "dos" and "don'ts" of gift-giving practices in China? You may need to write down at least three of them on the lines.

"dos"

____

____

____

____

"don'ts"

____

____

____

____

Task 2

In the following task, you are going to decide if the staff had done a proper job in gift-giving. Write "R" for right and "W" for wrong.

(1) ________ Send your British client a bunch of lilies.
(2) ________ Send your German client a gift with black wrapping.
(3) ________ Send your Latin American client a silk handkerchief.
(4) ________ Send your Korean client a clock as a gift.
(5) ________ Send your French client a precious gift to build your relationship.
(6) ________ Send your Thai client three sets of Yixing clay teapots.
(7) ________ Send your client a gift with your company logo as a thank-you gift.
(8) ________ Send your Arabian client a bottle of Moutai liquor.
(9) ________ Send your Japanese client a gift with white wrapping.
(10) ________ Send your Korean clients gifts at the very beginning of negotiations.
(11) ________ Send your German clients gifts at the kickoff of negotiations.
(12) ________ Present your gifts with both hands to show your utmost respect to your clients.

3.2 Gift Receiving

Task 1

Think about the question critically: How will you respond when a colleague or a business partner gives you a present?

Task 2

Work in groups, conduct a study on how to receive gifts properly in China, and another country you plan to visit on business. Compare and note down the similarities and differences.

Cross Cultural Gift Receiving Etiquette		
	China	**Your Target Country: ________**
Similarities		
Differences		

Task 3

Your foreign client is leaving soon and you decide to buy him/her a present, but what to buy and how to send the present? Please work in pairs to role play the situation. You may use some visual aids or props to liven up the performance.

Section Ⅲ. Evaluation

Aspects of Learning Performance		Rating				
		1	2	3	4	5
1	I have deepened my understanding of business reception.					
2	I can master common English vocabulary and skills related to business reception.					
3	I can write formal invitation letters in English.					
4	I can identify the major differences of invitation letters between China and other cultures.					
5	I can use right address forms and greetings in English to introduce each other.					
6	I can exchange business card in an appropriate manner.					
7	I understand the concept of power distance and can use it in identifying position and status.					
8	I understand the differences of dining customs between China and UK.					
9	I can make seating arrangement in Chinese and British way.					
10	I can give gifts to customers from another culture and take cultural taboos into consideration.					
Remarks						

Section Ⅳ. Reflection and Summary

Unit 2 Business Meeting

PPT

Section Ⅰ. Task Steps and Requirements

NO.	Steps	Requirements	Others
1	Before Meeting	1. Know the concept of high-context culture and low-context culture. 2. Be able to determine the formality of a culture. 3. Know the importance of a fixer and determine if a fixer is necessary according to the actual situation. 4. Be able to draft the meeting agenda according to the objectives of the meeting, the participants and other important factors. 5. Be able to arrange the seats for each participant.	
2	During Meeting	1. Know the different meanings of "punctuality" based on cultural differences. 2. Can use proper verbal expressions and body language to make introduction and greet each other. 3. Know the business card rituals and can design a business card of your own. 4. Know the importance of an interpreter during the meeting. 5. Can communicate effectively with your interpreter.	
3	After Meeting	1. Be able to summarize the key information of a meeting. 2. Can evaluate the meeting and make suggestions on how to improve the follow-up meeting.	

Section Ⅱ. Task Scenario

You are working in a Chinese pharmaceutical company which is planning to hold a business meeting to initiate the international cooperation with a foreign company, and you are going to prepare for this meeting. Please consider the intercultural differences between the two countries.

1. Before Meeting

1.1 Terminology and Theories

(1) What's your understanding of high-context culture and low-context culture?

(2) Classify the countries in the box into high-context or low-context culture respectively.

Republic of Korea	Argentina	Russia	China	Australia
Saudi Arabia	Japan	USA	Germany	Canada

High-context cultural countries:

____

____

____

Low-context cultural countries:

____

____

____

(3) In addition to determining whether a culture is high-context or low-context, there are other perspectives we can consider to understand how people from that culture interact with others in terms of formality and informality. What are they?

(4) Certain rules should be followed when conducting a business meeting with partners from other cultures. Please read these rules in the first column of the following table and fill in the blanks with "Yes" if the rule should be obeyed in the corresponding culture and write "No" if not.

Rules	High-Context Culture	Low-Context Culture
Written invitation		
Third-party introduction		
Detailed statistics in the first meeting		

1.2 Making Preparation

Task

Think about the following questions critically:

(1) Which form of communication is the more reliable one, telephone or written correspondence?

(2) Do you think it's important to consult a fixer before the meeting?

1.3 Drafting the Agenda

Meeting agenda is a schedule for your meeting arrangement. Drafting an agenda beforehand can lead to a more efficient and productive meeting.

Task 1

In order to design a practical and helpful meeting agenda, you need to know what should be involved and what needs to be taken into account. Therefore, in this task, you are going to learn how to draft a meeting agenda by following some steps listed below. In each step, you need to think critically, discuss the given questions thoroughly with your partner.

Step 1	**Identify the objectives of meeting** Read the two objectives below, and decide which one is more appropriate and give your reasons: Objective 1: to approve the company's monthly advertising budget Objective 2: to optimize overall spending
Step 2	**Ask participants for input** Why is it necessary to ask participants for input? What information do you need from participants?
Step 3	**List the questions you want to address** Why is it more important to list questions under a certain topic rather than just put a topic on the agenda?
Step 4	**Identify the purpose of each task** Why is it significant to remind participants the purpose of each task or to help them to identify the purpose of each task?

to be continued

continued

Step 5	**Estimate the amount of time to spend on each topic** What factors should be taken into account when estimating each topic's time consumption?
Step 6	**Identify who leads each topic** What are the possible advantages of assigning different participants to lead different topics?
Step 7	**End each meeting with a review** What elements should be included in the review?

Task 2

Scenario:

Your company is going to host the business meeting at 2 p. m. on next Monday (April 1, 20××) in the major meeting room of the company. You are assigned to set a meeting agenda. After contacting and consulting with other participants, you have drawn up a couple of topics to discuss during the meeting.

Please read the following two drafts and tell what elements are missing. Work with your group members to improve them.

Meeting Agenda 1

Date: Time: Location:

Topic 1: Title of the first topic

Point 1: XXXXXX

Point 2: XXXXXX

Point 3: XXXXXX

Topic 2: Title of the second topic

Point 1: XXXXXX

Point 2: XXXXXX

Point 3: XXXXXX

Topic 3: Title of the third topic

Point 1: XXXXXX

Point 2: XXXXXX

Point 3: XXXXXX

Conclusion

Meeting Agenda 2

Date: Location: Time:

Opening-up	**15 mins**
Topic 1: Title of the first topic Step 1: leader brings the topic Step 2: free discussion Step 3: participants present ideas Step 4: leader concludes	**20 mins**
Topic 2: Title of the second topic Step 1: leader brings the topic Step 2: free discussion Step 3: participants present ideas Step 4: leader concludes	**20 mins**
Topic 3: Title of the third topic Step 1: leader brings the topic Step 2: free discussion Step 3: participants present ideas Step 4: leader concludes	**20 mins**

1.4 Seating Arrangement

Task 1

The following are some rules of business seating arrangements. Complete these rules by ticking (√) the right word in each bracket:

Rule No. 1: (Guests/Hosts) are usually in a more important position.

Rule No. 2: People who are facing the door usually enjoy (higher/lower) priority.

Rule No. 3: Both parties should sit (opposite/next) to each other.

Rule No. 4: People of different gender should sit (together/apart).

Rule No. 5: Right is right, and then is left. It means the (right/left) side is regarded more important than the one on the (right/left) side.

Task 2

Scenario 1:

The president and vice-president of ABC Corporation Limited in USA are going to visit China. The manager and secretary from Guangming Company in China are going to attend the meeting with them.

(1) Based on the rules presented in Task 1, please determine the most important person in this scenario.

(2) There is a picture of the meeting room shown below. Please discuss with your group members and arrange the seats for each person. Write their titles in the proper positions.

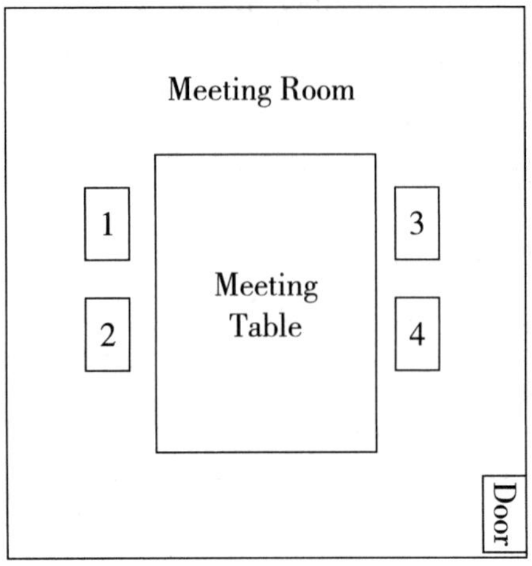

Position 1: ______________________ Position 3: ______________________

Position 2: ______________________ Position 4: ______________________

Scenario 2:

Visitors from ABC Corporation Limited in USA are going to attend a meeting hosted by your company. You are assigned to make place cards based on the attendees listed below. Also, you will need to put all these place cards in the right positions.

Attendees List			
Attendees from ABC Company		**Attendees from Your Company**	
Name	**Title**	**Name**	**Title**
Mr. Smith	President	Ms. Zhao	President
Mr. Johnson	Sales Manager	Miss. Wu	Secretary
Mr. Green	Sales Representative	Ms. Liu	Sales Manager
Ms. Cutler	Sales Manager	Mr. Wang	Sales Manager
Miss. Evans	Sales Representative	Mr. Han	Sales Representative

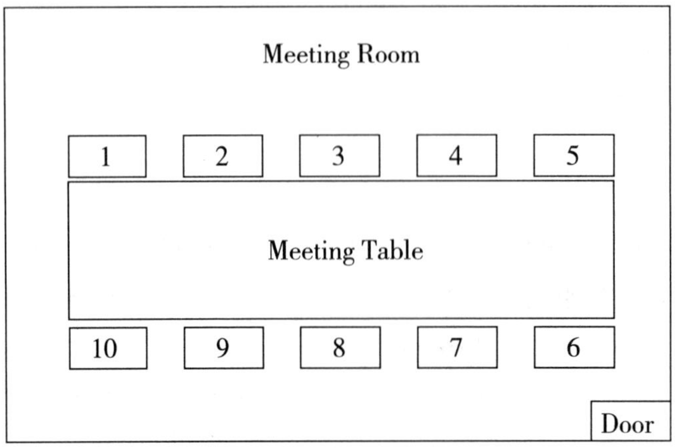

Position 1. ______________________ Position 6. ______________________

Position 2. ______________________ Position 7. ______________________

Position 3. ______________________ Position 8. ______________________

Position 4. ______________________ Position 9. ______________________

Position 5. ______________________ Position 10. ______________________

Task 3

In Unit 1, we have learned the seating arrangement rules in business dining. Can you summarize the similarities and differences in seating arrangement between business dining and business meeting?

2. During Meeting

2.1 Being Punctual

In most cultures, punctuality is essential especially in a formal meeting.

Task 1

You are going to interview at least 5 people with different ages, genders, occupations and nationalities. Please fill the results in the table below.

Interview question: What time will you arrive at the meeting room if there is an important meeting at 9 o'clock tomorrow morning?

Interviewee (Describe the Interviewee)	Arriving Time
1.	
2.	
3.	
4.	
5.	

Task 2

Read the following statements and decide whether they are true(T) or false(F).

(1) ________ It is wise to give yourself sufficient time to adjust before any meeting.

(2) ________ Some countries like USA and UK have rather strict demand for being punctual.

(3) ________ Always build in extra time on your way to the meeting.

(4) ________ People of different cultures share the same concept of punctuality.

(5) ________ Arabians and Latin Americans tend to be late for business meetings.

2.2 Introductions and Greetings

Task

Match the countries in the left column with the rituals of greetings and introductions in the right column.

Countries	Rituals of Greetings and Introductions
India	Bowing
USA	Men often exchange kisses on the right cheek
Japan	Shaking hands
Saudi Arabia	Hands shake and extra pat on the back
France	Both hands holding together in a prayerful position

2.3 Business Card Rituals

Task 1

Think about the following questions critically:

(1) Do you think it is proper to send your business card to an Indian customer with your left hand? Why or why not?

(2) Why do Japanese businessmen take a formal attitude towards the business card ritual?

(3) How to exchange business cards properly in Japan?

(4) Why is business card etiquette quite casual in USA and Europe?

(5) What are the basic elements of a business card?

(6) If you are facing a multitude of guests, in what order should you present your business card?

(7) Is it necessary to have one side of your business card translated into another language? Why or why not?

(8) Why does the literal translation of business titles may lead to misunderstandings?

Task 2

Scenario:

你是光明医疗器械有限公司的销售副经理，你将代表公司接待来访的美国客人，请设计双语名片为接待任务做准备。

Front side:

Back side:

Task 3

The American visitors have just arrived at the meeting room, you are going to greet them, make the introduction and exchange your business cards. Please role play the situation.

2.4 Interpreters: Key to Success

Task 1

Work in groups and discuss the questions below:

(1) During the meeting, do you think it's wise to have a bilingual employee on your team even if profes-

sional interpreters are in place? Why or why not?

(2) During the meeting, what other messages should be translated apart from the literal meaning of the speaker?

(3) As a visitor with no employee familiar with the native language or culture of the host country, is it advisable to accept the employee of the host company as your interpreter?

Task 2

There are some tips for hiring and communicating with interpreters. Please add the headings for each of the tips below:

(1) ______________________________

You need to screen and test your interpreters to make sure that they are professional in technical language and idioms of your business field. Also, knowing the local dialect will be a plus.

(2) ______________________________

If the discussions during the meeting are highly specialized, it is recommended to provide your interpreter with a glossary of special terms he or she may need during the meeting/negotiation.

(3) ______________________________

Hold a discussion with your interpreter before the meeting to get familiar with each other's speaking styles and turn-taking signals, like when to stop for interpretation.

(4) ______________________________

During the meeting, remind yourself of pausing for interpretation and stick to the main idea. It is impolite to resume your talking when the interpreter is still translating, and be patient as interpretation may lengthen the meeting time. Set resting time for interpreters every couple of hours.

(5) ______________________________

Never arrange an interpreter to sit in a major position in the meeting table or a seat between speakers of two sides. The speakers should not talk to the interpreter while speaking. Instead, they should look at the foreign associates they are talking to. What's more, speakers need to lower their speed and deliver their meanings more explicitly.

(6) ______________________________

It is the counterpart, not the interpreter who exchanges ideas with you, so always focus on the body language and facial expressions of your counterpart instead of the interpreter.

(7) ______________________________

When each side has their own interpreter, the interpreters should only translate what their own team is talking about. The interpreters should not interrupt each other or speak over each other.

(8) ______________________________

If you are not satisfied with the job done by your interpreter, do not criticize him/her in front of your counterpart, as the action may be misinterpreted as dissension on your part. If you need to be critical, do it in private.

(9) ______________________________

Double check the literal meanings and some nonverbal messages like para-languages with your interpreter at the end of each session of the meeting, in case there is any confusion which may cause semantic misunderstandings.

3. After Meeting

Task

Based on what you have learned in this unit, please work in groups and discuss the following questions:

(1) Why are some meetings successful and others failed? What are the features of a successful meeting?

(2) Write some tips for effective meetings based on your discussion.

Section Ⅲ. Evaluation

Aspects of Learning Performance		Rating				
		1	2	3	4	5
1	I have deepened my understanding of intercultural meeting.					
2	I can determine the formality of a culture based on the concept of high-context and low-context culture.					
3	I can draft an effective meeting agenda.					
4	I am able to arrange the seat for each participant in a meeting.					
5	I know punctuality may not mean the same in different cultures.					
6	I am able to make an introduction and greet each other in formal occasions.					
7	I know the business card ritual in different cultures and can perform business card exchange accordingly.					
8	I am able to communicate effectively with the interpreter during the meeting.					
9	I am able to note down and summarize the key information of a meeting.					
10	I can evaluate the effectiveness of a meeting and make suggestions on how to make an improvement.					
Remarks						

Section Ⅳ. Reflection and Summary

PPT

Unit 3　Business Negotiation

Section Ⅰ. Task Steps and Requirements

NO.	Steps	Requirements	Others
1	Before Negotiation	1. Know the importance of negotiation team and can select the right people to build a negotiation team. 2. Be able to build relationship in business negotiation. 3. Be able to draft an effective negotiation agenda. 4. Be able to profile your negotiation counterparty and adopt the right negotiation strategy accordingly.	
2	During Negotiation	1. Know the different ways of initiating a negotiation. 2. Can use different ways to convince your negotiation counterparty. 3. Know different conflict resolutions based on cultural differences. 4. Can apply various ways of negotiation skills into practical use. 5. Can use the "if" language to make concessions.	
3	After Negotiation	Be able to improve your negotiation skills by reviewing the process of negotiation.	

Section Ⅱ. Task Scenario

You are working in the Sales Department of a Chinese medical device company. The Sales Director is planning to sell a new model of medical device to a foreign company. You are assigned to prepare for the negotiation.

1. Before Negotiation

1.1 Terminology and Theories

(1) What is your understanding of negotiation?

(2) What may happen during the process of intercultural negotiation without knowing the cultural differences of negotiators?

(3) How do you define "a successful negotiation"?

(4) As a universal concept, "face" contains different meanings in different countries and cultures. Please compare and explain the differences between Chinese "face" and American "face".

(5) What do you know about "win-win" situation and zero-sum mentality in the process of negotiation?

1.2 Team Selection

Task 1

The first thing in team selection is to determine the team size. Please conduct a discussion with your partner and decide how many of your members will attend the negotiation.

Task 2

Negotiators are normally selected based on the criteria listed below. Please work in groups to discuss about each criterion and fill in the form to explain why you think each criterion is important.

Negotiating Experience	
Status (age, rank, gender, etc.)	
Knowledge of the Subject	
Personality (faithfulness, affability, etc.)	

1.3 Relationship Building

Building relationship in business negotiation means spending time to get acquainted with the person you conduct business with.

Read the following statements and decide if they are true(T) or false(F).

(1) ________ Building relationships before negotiations is not significant in Hispanic countries.

(2) ________ You may need an intermediary in the process of relationship-building with an Argentinean company.

(3) ________ Having tea and chatting may considered as a waste of time between an Indian and an American.

(4) ________ In Central and Eastern Europe, the essential part of building relationship is making introductions.

(5) ________ Since Arabs build commercial partnerships with friends only, it is necessary to establish a friendship with them before conducting a business.

(6) ________ In Asian countries, building a relationship with potential business partner is not a necessity, so it is advisable to locate an agent to serve as an intermediary.

1.4 Negotiation Agenda

Task 1

Do you think it is necessary to prepare a negotiation agenda? Discuss with your partner and present your ideas in class.

Task 2

A negotiation agenda is welcomed in some countries but may not be taken up in others. Please conduct a study, have a discussion with your partner and put the country names into proper columns. (USA, Columbia, Saudi Arabia, Japan, UK)

Countries Prefer a Negotiation Agenda	Countries Prefer Not to Have a Negotiation Agenda

Task 3

What elements should be involved in a negotiation agenda? Brainstorm as many ideas as possible, then design a negotiation agenda and present it in tabular form.

1.5 More on Negotiation Preparation

Task 1

Read the following statements and decide if they are True(T) or False(F).

(1) You should be familiar with the ranking system of the other company and know who can cut the deal in their company.

(2) Know well about the policy of the other company.

(3) List all your needs and wants together, which may help you to present them during the negotiation.

(4) Past is past, circumstances are changing every second. So every negotiation is a brand new battle to fight for.

(5) Go to the records and learn from all negotiation cases which may help you for the upcoming one.

Task 2

Select a country as your research object. Prepare a negotiation profile for people from that country who will be negotiating with representatives from your company. Include information in the following table.

Aspects for Consideration	Your Findings
Task-driven or relationship-driven	
High-context or low-context	
What role of "face"	
What is their concept of "time horizon"	
Direct or indirect communication style	
Zero-sum or win-win strategy	
Communication style of major negotiators	
Top-down or bottom-up decision-making process	
Formal agreement or agreement in principle	

2. During Negotiation

2.1 Small Talk

Task

Small talk is usually considered as an effective way to break the ice and a prelude to a negotiation. However, people from countries like Finland prefer not to engage in small talk and get down to business immediately. Please conduct a group study to see if there is any other country that is similar to Finland in terms of small talk and figure out the underlying reasons.

2.2 Information Exchange

Task

Discuss with your teammates: what methods can you think of to obtain information from your negotiation counterparty?

2.3 Framing Your Questions

Asking questions is an important part of gaining information. However, it could be risky if the questions are presented inappropriately.

Task

Revise the following questions to make them less aggressive and rewrite them on the lines below.

(1) Where did you get that unit price?

(2) What is your preference of packing?

(3) Why did you offer me a higher unit price than last year?

(4) How many do you want to order for the next season?

Rewrite:

(1) ____

____

____

(2) ____

____

____

(3) ____

____

____

(4) ____

____

____

2.4 Persuasion or Debate

Task 1

Generally, there are two methods to convince your counterparty during the negotiation: persuasion and debate. Please work in groups and discuss which one is more suitable, and give your reasons.

Task 2

The following three examples represent two basic approaches of persuasion—logical and emotional, which are commonly adopted in negotiation. Please read them carefully and decide which example is logical and which is emotional.

Example 1:

According to the data we collected, our exports will reach 20 million Yuan next year, a year-on-year increase of 30 percent. It will be necessary to purchase 30% more raw material from your company this year. What's more, our purchasing amount will increase yearly and we can sign a long-term contract if the price is 10% lower.

Example 2:

Dear manager, we are a company with history, we have a good reputation in payments which you can see in the last a couple of transactions. What we are looking for is a long-term relationship between two companies. However, a reasonable price is necessary for convincing our procurement manager to make the deal. So we hope we can come to an agreement on the 10% decrease of the unit price.

Example 3:

My deer partner, after our 5-year cooperation, you must have fully realized that we are a very good supplier, the price we offer to your company is always the best one and our quality is stable. You know, production cost is increasing, such as the material and labor cost, but we have never increased the price for your company. We believe the value of our product justifies its price, I'm afraid we have to stand by the price we have set.

Task 3

Scenario:

If you are the buyer or seller in Example 1, 2 or 3 above, how will you response? Please pick one example and write down your response.

____

____

____

____

____

2.5 Conflict Resolution

Task 1

Negotiators from different cultures (individualistic or collectivistic) have different ideologies on mission completion or a successful negotiation. That is how conflicts occur. In this task, you are going to do your research first, find out the differences between collectivistic culture and individualistic culture, know people from which culture is more task-driven and which is more relationship-driven, and then fill in the blanks with the words in the box.

collectivistic	task-driven	individualistic	relationship-driven

During the negotiations, people from ________ cultures prefer to avoid the risks, while people from ________ cultures tend to confront with the conflicts as they believe confrontation is an efficient way to settle problems.

In ________ cultures, negotiators tend to close the deal during the meeting, but in ________ cultures, negotiators are more willing to build the relationship with the counterparty first.

Task 2

Based on the information presented in the task above, please explain the two terms below.

High risk-avoidance culture

____

____

Low risk-avoidance culture

____

____

2.6 Decision Making

Decision making process varies from culture to culture. In some collectivistic cultures, a decision should be made with consensus of all staff; while in most individualistic cultures, the leader alone can make the decision for the company. In this case, please compare the two decision making process—Top-down and Bottom-up, and see if there are any advantages and disadvantages of them respectively and fill in the form below.

	Top-Down Approach	Bottom-Up Approach
Advantages		
Disadvantages		

2.7 Concession and Agreement

Task 1

Signing a contract or reaching an agreement usually marks the end of a negotiation. However, without giving some concessions, it is unlikely to reach a final agreement. An experienced negotiator tends to use the "if" language as a negotiating tactic. The following is an example of how to use the "if" language. Read this example and give your response to the rest of statements by using the "if" language.

Example 1:

A: We insist that the payment method should be L/C.

B: We will accept your payment method if you'll agree to a 10% discount on future orders.

Example 2:

A: We are looking forward to starting with a trial order with bulk price.

B: We can offer you with that price if you pay by T/T for this order.

Example 3:

A: This is an urgent order, and we need it in 15 days.

B: We can manage to do that if we can make the color and quality confirmation in 3 days, and you can book the shipment by your own.

A: We need 1, 000 yards and 200 yards for each color.

B: As a trial order, we can arrange the production for you if ______________________________

____

____

____

A: Packing with our label will be preferred in this trail order.

B: It's not a big deal if ______________________________

____

____

____

A: We need the color strike in 3 days.

B: It will be ready tomorrow if ______________________________

____

____

____

Task 2

The effectiveness of a contract may vary from countries and cultures as people from different regions hold different attitudes toward it.

So, please conduct a study in groups, find and compare some views on contract based on reliable sources and examples.

Step 1: Fulfill the form below.

Countries	Views on Contract	Reference
USA		
France		
Japan		

to be continued

continued

Countries	Views on Contract	Reference
Germany		
Egypt		
Argentina		

Step 2: Can you relate the views on contract to the culture? Explain the rationale behind it.

Step 3: What will you do if the contract view of your counterparty is different from yours? Pick one contract view and share your idea.

3. After Negotiation

Task

Make a group discussion based on the following questions. Give some suggestions on how to improve one's negotiation skills.

(1) Will you make the first move during the negotiation? Why?

(2) Clear statements and simple language are recommended during the negotiation. Do you know why?

(3) Do you think it is important to anticipate the conditions or offers which may be proposed by the other company? And why?

(4) As a customer or investor, is there any benefit you can take from the position?

(5) As the decision maker of your team, what would you do if the two parties cannot reach a deal?

Section Ⅲ. Evaluation

Aspects of Learning Performance		Rating				
		1	2	3	4	5
1	I have deepened my understanding of intercultural negotiation.					
2	I can select the right people to build a negotiation team.					
3	I can draft an effective negotiation agenda.					
4	I am able to profile my negotiation counterparty and adopt the right negotiation strategy accordingly.					
5	I can initiate the negotiation in a right way.					
6	I am able to use the right way to convince my negotiation counterparty.					
7	I know different ways to resolve conflicts based on cultural differences.					
8	I can use the "if" language to make concessions when necessary.					
9	I am able to apply various ways of negotiation skills into practical use.					
10	I am able to improve my negotiation skills by reviewing the process of negotiation.					
Remarks						

Section Ⅳ. Reflection and Summary

Unit 4 Marketing Planning

PPT

Section Ⅰ. Task Steps and Requirements

NO.	Steps	Requirements	Others
1	Before Planning	1. Be able to clearly state your marketing objectives. 2. Be able to use various methods to conduct market research. 3. Be able to collect information about your product, your customers and your competitors.	
2	Making a Plan	1. Understand SWOT Analysis and can apply it in product analysis. 2. Be able to decide your distribution strategy in the target market. 3. Be able to decide your brand name for the target market by taking cultural elements into consideration. 4. Be able to decide your slogan and avoid the taboos in the target market. 5. Be able to design your product appearance for the target market. 6. Understand different pricing strategies and can apply them in your marketing.	
3	After Planning	Think about how traditional Chinese medicine goes global.	

Section Ⅱ. Task Scenario

You are with a Chinese Liang Cha (herbal beverage) company which is planning to expand the overseas market and promote its core product. As a member of the marketing department, you are assigned to draft a marketing plan of the herbal beverage named 碧霞 for the discussion next Monday and you need to take intercultural differences into account.

1. Before Planning

1.1 Terminology and Theories

(1) What is SWOT Analysis?

(2) What distribution methods do you know?

(3) How many advertising media can you think of?

(4) What cultural elements do you suppose to consider when designing your product appearance and packaging?

1.2 Your Objectives

Task

Setting an objective is necessary and beneficial for your marketing plan. Please conduct a discussion with your partner and decide which of the following objectives are effective and which are not, and explain why.

(1) To attract new customers in the target market.

(2) To increase the number of new users by 10% in the target market within the next 12 months.

(3) To improve the customer satisfaction and loyalty.

(4) To achieve a repurchase rate of 60% among new users within the next 12 months.

(5) To increase the market share to 5% in the target market before next quarter.

1.3 Collecting Information

Collecting information upon detailed research is essential before developing your plan. Therefore, in this part, you are going to collect information for your marketing plan based on the following tasks.

Task 1

Get an insight about your product through the following steps:

Step 1: Before promoting, you need to know your product well. Usually we use SWOT analysis to assess business competition. SWOT is a strategic planning technique that outlines a product's strengths, weaknesses, opportunities, and threats. Please take a SWOT analysis of your product and fill out the table below. ("its" refers to your product's)

Its Strengths	
Its Weaknesses	
Its Opportunities	
Its Threats	

Step 2: The analytical table below may help you know better about your product from the perspective of culture. Please fill it out based on your research.

Chinese Name of the Product	
Meaning of the Name	
Meaning of the Logo	
History of the Product	
Efficacy of the Product	

to be continued

continued

Product Appearance	
Special Features	
Slogan	
Flavor	

Task 2

Do research on your target customers. You may conduct your survey based on the table below.

Attitudes toward Chinese Herbal Product	
Taste Preference	
Color Preference	
Color Taboos	
Open-Minded or Conservative	
What Kind of Chinese Cultural Element(s) Do They Prefer	

Task 3

Identifying your competitors is a crucial step before entering a new market. Please compare your products and your competitors' by filling the table below. ("their" refers to your competitor's in the table)

	Competitor 1	**Competitor 2**
Similarities		

to be continued

continued

	Competitor 1	Competitor 2
Differences		
Their Strengths and Weaknesses		
Customers' Ideas about Their Products		
Their Pricing Strategy		

Task 4

Think about the following questions critically:

What do you think of your competitors' strengths and weaknesses? Can you give some suggestions on improving their weaknesses?

2. Making a Plan

2.1 Distribution Strategy

Task

Please follow the steps below to decide your distribution strategy in the target market.

Step 1: Distribution strategy here means how you get your products into the hands of your customers. There are some common direct marketing methods for your consideration, which are: home delivery, open markets, mail order, internet sales, pick your own (U-pick), etc. Conduct a research and discuss in groups and decide which one(s) will be the proper option(s) in your target market.

Step 2: You may also need to consider an indirect selling strategy of using the local retailers for your products distribution. Conduct a research and find right retailers as your ideal distributors.

Step 3: Conduct a comprehensive comparison and analysis on the distribution methods mentioned in the previous two steps, pick one or several methods to draw up a distribution plan in the target market based on the table you are going to fill out below.

Distribution Methods	Proportion of Total Sales (%)	
Direct distribution methods	home delivery	
	open markets mail order	
	internet sales	
	U-pick	
	others:	
Indirect distribution methods	retailer 1:	
	retailer 2:	
	retailer 3:	

2.2 Promotion Strategy

Task 1

Please follow the steps below to decide your brand name for the target market.

Step 1: A brand name offers the first impression to the customers. In this task, you are going to look at the failed brand names below, discuss with your partner to explain why.

Original Brand Name	Target Market	Failed Brand Name
Goldlion	Hong Kong, China	金狮
Sprite	Hong Kong, China	十必利
Chevy Nova (General Motors)	Latin American countries	Nova
紫罗兰（男装）	USA	Violet
蓝天（牙膏）	USA	BlueSky
蝙蝠（电扇）	USA	Bat

Step 2: Discuss with your partner, think about the issues you should pay attention to when naming a product

in the language of your target market and share your ideas with your group members.

Step 3: Discuss in groups, how will you name your brand based on its Chinese name (碧霞)? Do you think it's better to translate the Chinese brand name into English, or translate it based on its Chinese meaning, or rename it to fit the preference of your target customers? Share the name you decide along with the rationales behind it.

Task 2

Please follow the steps below to decide your slogan for the target market.

Step 1: As a fundamental element of product promotion, slogan is meant to be attractive, impressive, and most importantly it can increase the consumption rate. However, with translation errors caused by ignorance of intercultural differences, some slogans may lead to a failed advertising campaign.

Please look at the failed slogans below, discuss with your partner and explain why.

Brand	**Target Market**	**Failed Slogan**
Pepsi	China	Brings you back to life. (original version) 百事可乐将死去的祖先从坟墓中带回来。(translated version)
Electrolux	USA	Nothing sucks like an Electrolux.
KFC	China	It's Finger Lickin'Good. (original version) 吃掉你的手指头。(translated version)
HSBC	Some non-English speaking countries	Assume nothing. (original version) Do nothing. (translated version)
Orange	North Ireland	The future's bright, the future's Orange.

Step 2: There are many successful cases of advertising slogans listed below. Please work in groups, find out their Chinese versions and try to explain: why did these slogans succeed?

Successful English slogans:

Tide: Tide's in, dirt's out.

Seven-up: Fresh up with Seven-up.

Toyota: Where there is a way for a car, there is a Toyota.

De Beers: A diamond lasts forever.

Ricoh: We lead, others copy.

Step 3: Discuss in groups, think about the issues you should pay attention to when designing or translating a slogan. Design an advertising slogan for your target market in both Chinese and English.

Task 3

Please follow the steps below to decide your product appearance for the target market.

Step 1: Before designing the appearance of a product or its packaging, knowing which colors to use is essential, and knowing which colors are preferred or disapproved in the culture of your target market is a priority. Therefore, in this part you are going to learn some of the disapproved colors in a certain culture based on the table below, and fill out the blanks concerning your target market.

Countries	Disapproved Color(s)	Reasons of Disapproval
China	white, black	colors of mourning
Argentina	light brown	color of mourning
Mexico	green, white, red	colors of national flag
Denmark	black, yellow	connotes falseness
Sudan	yellow	connotes sickness
Arabian countries	blue	relates to death
Latin American countries	purple	relates to death
(Your target market)		

Step 2: When designing the appearance of a product or its packaging, some objects or symbols are supposed to be avoided because of some cultural and historical reasons. Thus, in this section, you are going to learn some disapproved symbols in different countries based on the table below and fill out the blanks concerning your target market.

Countries	Disapproved Symbol(s)	Reasons of Disapproval
China	crow	a harbinger of death
Australia	the red rising sun	a reminder of Japan's colors in World War Ⅱ
UK	swastika	a symbol of Nazi
Hungary	cross and arrow	a reminder of the Arrow Cross party
Thailand	feet	regarded as despicable
European countries	black cat	associated with bad luck
(Your target market)		

Step 3: Based on your previous researches, think about the colors and symbols you should pay attention to when designing the appearance or packaging of your product for a certain market. Create your own design, give a rough description of your design and share it in the class.

Task 4

Till now, you have decided the brand name, the slogan and the appearance of your product. Please think about what media you will use to launch the advertising campaign. Present your ideas within class with the help of the instructions below:

(1) If you use an advertisement, write the text and do rough art work.

(2) If you use a TV commercial, use a storyboard to illustrate your idea.

(3) If you use a radio spot, write the script, add some sound effects.

(4) If you use other media, indicate what pictures, text, slogans will be used.

2.3 Pricing Strategy

Here are three common pricing strategies:

1. Cost-oriented pricing strategy: Add a specific percentage on your cost of production. For example, you may add 30% to your cost of production based on the market preference.

2. Flexible pricing strategy: Study for how your customers' preference or needs vary from time to time, and your price may change according to the season, time, temperature, etc.

3. Relative pricing strategy: Find the most attractive price of similar products in the market and set your own price based on it. You may also increase or lower the price based upon it.

Task:

Based on the three pricing strategies listed above, you are going to discuss with your partner to pick one of them first, then you need to consider the strategy with your cost of production. Also, you will need to compare it with your competitors' pricing strategies, make a final decision upon thorough consideration and share it in the class with reasons.

2.4 Making a Marketing Plan

Make your own marketing plan based on the worksheet below.

Marketing Plan Worksheet	
Executive summary (make a summary on what you meant to fulfill in this marketing plan)	

to be continued

continued

Marketing Plan Worksheet	
Your goals/objectives (talk about the goals/objects you meant to achieve)	
Your business (describe your business, including your industry, your product/service)	
Your market (describe the market and the customers you are going to serve)	
Your competitors (compare you and your products to your competitors and their products, analyze their strengths and weaknesses)	
Distribution strategy (find the best way to send your products to the hands of customers)	
Promotion (describe your packaging design, slogan and tell how you will let people know your product in the target market)	
Price (set a price for your product and tell the rationale behind)	

3. After Planning

The herbal beverage, as a branch of traditional Chinese medicine culture, enjoys a long history in China, and the use of herbs is a time-honored approach for strengthening the body and treating disease. However, due to various factors, traditional Chinese medicine culture still has a long way to go in the process of going global. Please think and discuss this question: How does traditional Chinese medicine go global?

Section Ⅲ. Evaluation

Aspects of Learning Performance		Rating				
		1	2	3	4	5
1	I have deepened my understanding of marketing planning.					
2	I can clearly state my marketing objectives.					
3	I am able to use various methods to conduct market research.					
4	I am able to collect information about my product, my customers and my competitors.					
5	I understand SWOT Analysis and can apply it in product analysis.					
6	I am able to decide the distribution strategy in the target market.					
7	I am able to decide the brand name for the target market by taking cultural elements into consideration.					
8	I am able to decide my slogan and avoid the taboos in the target market.					
9	I am able to design my product appearance for the target market.					
10	I understand different pricing strategies and can apply them in my marketing planning.					
Remarks						

Section Ⅳ. Reflection and Summary

PPT

Unit 5 Job Interview

Section Ⅰ. Task Steps and Requirements

NO.	Steps	Requirements	Others
1	Before Interview	1. Be able to know your target company from the cultural perspective. 2. Be able to analyze the different requirements for resume and cover letter in different countries. 3. Be able to identify the specific requirements of the target company.	
2	During Interview	1. Understand the relevant theoretical knowledge of cross-cultural verbal communication and nonverbal communication. 2. Can analyze the differences in verbal communication behaviors and nonverbal communication behaviors between China and the target country. 3. Can comprehensively analyze the matters that may need attention during the interview process in the target company. 4. Be able to discover and analyze the interviewers' nonverbal behaviors.	
3	After Interview	1. Be able to contact with the Human Resource Manager to know the result of your interview. 2. Be able to negotiate on salary, leave, etc. by phone or letter.	

Section Ⅱ. Task Scenario

You will participate in an interview for a sales position of a multinational company in the pharmaceutical industry. Please prepare for the interview with relevant intercultural communication knowledge by accomplishing the tasks below.

1. Before Interview

1.1 Terminology and Theories

(1) What is cultural taboo?

(2) What kind of cultural taboos may affect an international interview?

(3) Why do you think it's important to pay attention to intercultural communication in job hunting?

1.2 Know Your Target Company from the Perspective of Cross Cultural Communication

Task

Please complete the following table by comparing and analyzing the cultural differences between the target company and its Chinese counterpart. You may consider the company values, the different cultural taboos, the cultural values, etc.

	Target Multinational Company	Its Chinese Counterpart
Countries		
Staff composition (gender, nationality, etc.)		
Corporate values		
Cultural taboos		

1.3 Clothing and Apparel

Task 1

Think about the following questions critically:

It's commonly seen that many people will spend some time and energy dressing up for the interview. Will you do the same? Why or why not?

Task 2

Complete the table according to the clothing taboos of the target country.

	Target Multinational Company	**Its Chinese Counterpart**
Hairstyle		
Necktie		
Clothing color		
Clothes		
Shoes		
Socks		
Buttons		
Makeup		

Task 3

Please complete the description of your outfit on the interview day in combination with Task 2.

Company Name	
Time and Place	
Description of Your Outfit	

1.4 Resume

A resume is always asked when you are applying for a job. However, companies with different cultures will ask for different information involved in applicants' resumes.

Therefore, in this part, you are going to compare different requirements between your target foreign company and its Chinese counterpart, which may help you prepare a proper resume.

Task 1

Think about the following questions critically:

(1) There are two common resume formats, one is based on chronological order, and the other is skill-based resume. What are the differences between the two?

(2) What is the common format of a time-based resume?

(3) What are the focuses of a skill-based resume? Which skills should be listed in the resume? How to prove that you have these skills?

(4) How do you view the behavior of embellishing resumes?

Task 2

Based on your understanding of the country where the company belongs to, please judge whether the following information is expected to see in your resume when applying for the job.

	Target Multinational Company	Its Chinese Counterpart
Name		
Gender		
Address		
Telephone number		
Email		
Date of birth		
Ethnic		
Marital status		
Number of children		

to be continued

continued

	Target Multinational Company	Its Chinese Counterpart
Parent information		
Names of siblings/children		
Name of spouse		
Place of birth		
Nationality		
Religious affiliation		
Education		
Employment history		
Diplomas/degrees/transcript		
Interests		
References		
Financial obligations		

Task 3

Explain the major differences of resumes between China and your target country based on the table you filled in Task 2.

Task 4

Prepare a resume to be sent to your target company and apply for the sales position.

1.5 Cover Letter

Cover letter is also known as application letter. A cover letter is attached to the resume in most job-applying cases. It may help you to add more information like why you choose the company, your strengths for the position, etc.

Task 1

Apart from the reasons for writing a cover letter listed above, what other purposes for writing a cover letter can you think of ? Please list them below.

1. ____________________

2. ____________________

3. ____________________

4. ____________________

5. ____________________

Task 2

Based on the above tasks, write a cover letter to supplement your resume.

2. During Interview

2.1 Terminology and Theories

(1) What is high-context communication and what is low-context communication?

(2) How to determine whether a culture favors a direct or indirect style in communication?

(3) What are the purposes of indirect communication?

(4) Are Chinese always more indirect than Americans? If yes, can you explain why? If no, can you give some counter examples?

(5) Which verbal style do you think is preferable in contemporary Chinese society, self-enhancement or self-effacement?

2.2 Analysis of Cross-Cultural Behavior in Cross-Cultural Interview

Task 1

Complete the table according to the common nonverbal communication differences, linguistic communication differences and cultural taboos in cross-cultural communications.

		Target Multinational Company	**Its Chinese Counterpart**
Verbal communication	high-context/low-context culture		
	linear/non-linear language		
	humor		
	interruption		
Nonverbal communication	smile		
	eye contact		
	nodding		
	time		
	volume		
	pitch		

Task 2

Think about the following questions critically:

(1) Do you know any gestures we often use that might be misunderstood by people from other cultures?

(2) How will you interpret the action of looking into someone's eyes? Will you consider it as honest or rude? What about its meaning in other different countries or cultures?

(3) What are the different ways of greetings in different cultures or countries, especially in the occasion of an interview? Make demonstrations if necessary.

Task 3

People from different cultures have different senses of time. Do you know how late is late if you are going to attend an interview, a class, or a party in China? And what will that be if you are in Mexico, UAE or other countries? Do your research, compare the differences, try to find out the underlying cultural values and share the information you collected with your partner.

Task 4

Make a list of matters that needs special attention in the interview according to the table in Task 1.

Job Interview Checklist	
1	
2	
3	
4	
5	
6	
7	
8	

Task 5

Summarize and interpret the interviewer's evaluation of your interview performance by analyzing the interviewer's nonverbal expressions with the help of the table in Task 1.

Nonverbal Language	Your Analysis

Task 6

Prepare an opening statement based on the information in Task 1.

____

____

____

____

____

Task 7

Please work in a small group and plan a mock interview based on what you have learned so far. You should read the table below, notice how your performance in the mock interview will be evaluated. Keep these categories in mind as you perform and watch your classmates' mock interviews.

	Group 1	Group 2	Group 3	Group 4
Verbal communication matches the culture of target country	1, 2, 3, 4, 5	1, 2, 3, 4, 5	1, 2, 3, 4, 5	1, 2, 3, 4, 5
Nonverbal communication matches the culture of target country	1, 2, 3, 4, 5	1, 2, 3, 4, 5	1, 2, 3, 4, 5	1, 2, 3, 4, 5
Language	1, 2, 3, 4, 5	1, 2, 3, 4, 5	1, 2, 3, 4, 5	1, 2, 3, 4, 5
Fluency	1, 2, 3, 4, 5	1, 2, 3, 4, 5	1, 2, 3, 4, 5	1, 2, 3, 4, 5
Overall rating	1, 2, 3, 4, 5	1, 2, 3, 4, 5	1, 2, 3, 4, 5	1, 2, 3, 4, 5
What aspects do you like?				
What could be improved?				

Note: 1 = lowest; 5 = highest

3. After Interview

Task

Think about the following questions critically:

(1) After the interview, do you think it's better to write a letter asking for feedback or a letter expressing your gratitude, and why?

(2) If you decide to reject the offer, how would you express your decision politely?

(3) How would you negotiate on salary, leave, etc. by phone or by letter with the human resource manager?

Section Ⅲ. Evaluation

Aspects of Learning Performance		Rating				
		1	2	3	4	5
1	I have deepened my understanding of job interview.					
2	I can master common English vocabulary and skills related to interview.					
3	I can grasp the possible dress taboos in the cross-cultural interview process.					
4	I am able to compare and analyze the linguistic and nonlinguistic differences in relevant scenes.					
5	I can master the different requirements of different countries and cultures on the content of resumes.					
6	I am able to participate in the interview in English.					
7	I know the differences between Chinese and English resumes and cover letters.					
8	I am able to complete my English resume and cover letter.					
9	I am able to consult and communicate with the human resource manager appropriately and politely.					
10	I am able to accept/reject an offer in an appropriate way.					
Remarks						

Section Ⅳ. Reflection and Summary

Unit 6 Escort Interpretation

PPT

Section Ⅰ. Classification and Requirements

NO.	Steps	Requirements	Others
1	Proverbs and Idioms	1. Be able to compare the different cultural images of the same object in Chinese and English. 2. Know about some common proverbs and idioms in English and can use them correctly. 3. Be able to translate English proverbs and idioms into Chinese and vice versa.	
2	Color Phrases	1. Know about the cultural connotations of common colors. 2. Can tell the differences of color phrases in Chinese and English in terms of cultural connotation. 3. Be able to use the color phrases correctly.	
3	Animal Phrases	1. Know about the cultural connotations of common animals. 2. Can tell the differences of animal phrases in Chinese and English in terms of cultural connotation. 3. Be able to use the animal phrases correctly.	
4	Botanic Phrases	1. Know about the cultural connotations of common plants. 2. Can tell the differences of botanic phrases in Chinese and English in terms of cultural connotation. 3. Be able to use the botanic phrases correctly.	
5	Numbers	1. Know about the cultural connotations of some numbers. 2. Can tell the differences of numbers in Chinese and English in terms of cultural connotation. 3. Be able to translate numbers correctly.	

Section Ⅱ. Classification of Escort Interpretation

1. Proverbs and Idioms

Task 1

Compare the following English and Chinese idioms and discuss the underlying cultural implications.

English Idioms	Chinese Idioms
He who would search for pearls must dive below.	不入虎穴，焉得虎子
It was packed like sardines.	人山人海
Fish begins to stink at the head.	上梁不正下梁歪
As dumb as an oyster.	守口如瓶

Task 2

Translate the following English idioms into Chinese and vise versa.

1. A smooth sea never makes a skillful mariner.

____

2. Keep one's head above water.

____

3. Living without an aim is like sailing without a compass.

____

4. 雨后春笋

____

5. 挥金如土

____

6. 掌上明珠

Task 3

Compare and discuss the meanings of "west wind" in the following two Chinese and English poems, try to explain the reasons from the perspective of geographic differences.

Chinese poem：古道西风瘦马，夕阳西下，断肠人在天涯。

—马致远《天净沙》

English poem：It's a warm wind, the west wind, full of birds' cries.

—The West Wind by John Masefield

Task 4

Firstly, you need to fill out the table with corresponding Chinese idioms for the English ones and vice versa (the words given in brackets may help you find the corresponding English idioms). Secondly, compare the English and Chinese idioms, and discuss the differences from the perspective of diet culture.

Better half an egg than empty shell.	
Better some of the pudding than none of a pie.	
a piece of cake	
a big cheese	
a hot potato	
Too much pudding will choke a dog.	
Meat is much but manner is more.	
Meat make and clothes shapes, but manner makes a man.	
生米煮成熟饭	
覆水难收	(milk)
掌上明珠	(apple)
泰然自若	(cucumber)
干预某事	(pie)
天无绝人之路	(bread)
民以食为天	(bread)
萝卜白菜各有所爱	(meat)

Task 5

Work in groups and conduct a research on the English idioms below to find out the stories behind them. Then you may need to find the corresponding Chinese idioms and note them down on the given lines. At last, you need to explain the idiom and share the origin story in groups.

1. burn one's boats

____

2. Promethean heat

____

3. leave no stone unturned

____

4. Odyssey

____

5. cherish a snake in one's bosom

____

6. a feather in your cap

____

7. birds of a feather

____

8. meet one's Waterloo

____

9. Achilles' heel

____

10. Pandora's box

____

Task 6

Fill in the blanks with idioms in the last task (Task 5).

1. They have a lot in common and always stick together for everything, they are ____________.

2. "Another full mark in mathematics? You are really good at numbers, don't you? Math is now ____________."

3. You will ____________ someday if you maintain your style of doing things and never change.

4. If you are really tempted to take up that job offer in Beijing, you have to ____________.

5. I don't not know how far this ____________ will take us, but nothing will stop us.

6. It is still a myth as where he got the ____________ to create such a masterpiece.

2. Color Phrases

The word "color" contains meanings beyond the denotation of a certain color that can be observed, and its connotations may vary from culture to culture. In this section, you are going to learn, compare and practice different connotations of colors between Chinese and English-speaking cultures.

Task 1

Translate the following color phrases, think about the connotations of the color in each phrase and fill out the form below.

Colors	Phrases	Your Translation	Connotations in English	Connotations in Chinese
red	red ideas			
	a red battle			
	red alert			

to be continued

continued

Colors	Phrases	Your Translation	Connotations in English	Connotations in Chinese
red	red tape			
	red handed			
	see red			
	red hat			
	a red waste of his youth			
yellow	yellow journalism			
	yellow dog			
	yellow ribbons			
	yellow book			
	yellow pages			
green	a green age			
	a green hand			
	green-eyed			
	green table			
	green power			
	a green wound			

to be continued

continued

Colors	Phrases	Your Translation	Connotations in English	Connotations in Chinese
blue	blue video/film			
	blue blood			
	blue book			
	blue mood			
	a blue Monday			
	once in a blue moon			
	blue coat			
white	white soul			
	a white wedding			
	a white day			
	days marked with a white stone			
	a white lie			
	a white war			
	white hand			
	a white man			
black	a black day			
	a black dog			
	black sheep			
	black deed			
	black hearted			
	a black look			

Task 2

Translate the following Chinese color phrases into English.

红色

1. 红火________________

2. 红白喜事________________

3. 红娘________________

4. 红运________________

黄色

1. 黄色杂志________________

2. 黄毛丫头________________

3. 黄昏________________

4. 黄袍________________

绿色

1. 红男绿女________________

2. 绿窗________________

3. 绿林好汉________________

4. 戴绿帽子________________

蓝色

1. 青出于蓝________________

2. 蓝本________________

3. 蓝图________________

白色

1. 白费力气________________

2. 白脸________________

3. 白开水________________

4. 白手起家________________

5. 白眼________________

6. 清白________________

黑色

1. 黑心________________

2. 黑名单________________________________

3. 黑幕________________________________

4. 黑钱________________________________

5. 黑帮________________________________

Task 3

Use appropriate color phrases given in Task 1 to fill in the blanks in the sentences below. Some colors may be used more than once.

1. She showed up out of ________________ and surprised every one of us.

2. You look so ________________ this morning, are you all right?

3. He got a ________________ look from his mother as he got up late again and missed the school bus.

4. A difficult person like him must be a ________________ sheep of his family.

5. Even a ________________ lie may harm our feelings in some circumstances.

6. He is a man with ________________ soul who would never do anything harmful.

7. It was the first time I saw this gentleman saw ________________.

8. The application involves a lot of ________________ tape, so I decide to give up.

9. You can find the contact information of the company in the ________________ pages.

10. I treat him so well, but he end up cheating on me, what a ________________ dog!

11. Jealousy is a ________________ eye monster: it gets inside people, eats them up.

12. He's still a ________________ hand, don't be so critical of him.

3. Animal Phrases

The connotation of an animal is largely determined by culture. A certain animal may have a good reputation in one culture and may be subject to discrimination in another. Therefore, in this section, you are going to learn, compare and practice different connotations of animals between Chinese and Western cultures.

Task 1

In Chinese and Western cultures, some animals have similar or even the same connotation, while others do not. So please classify the given animals into two catalogs by filling out the box below.

dog	rat	dragon	wolf	fox
monkey	snake	owl	turtle	bat
eagle	horse	silkworm	crane	phoenix
peacock	cat			

Share Similar Connotation in Chinese and English	Have Different Connotations in Chinese and English

Task 2

Translate the following English animal phrases into Chinese.

1. raining cats and dogs

____

2. Love me, love my dog.

____

3. an old dog

____

4. Every dog has its day.

____

5. the swan song

____

6. do a rat

____

7. smell a rat

8. dirty rat

9. a drowned rat

10. in sheep's clothing

11. dragon lady

12. dragon's teeth

13. get one's monkey up

14. make a monkey out of someone

15. Monkey see, monkey do.

16. lion-hearted

17. work like a horse

____

18. talk a horse

____

19. neither fish or fowl

____

20. paper tiger

____

21. a bird's view

____

22. bull market

____

23. ostrich policy

____

24. the frog in the well

____

25. a dog's head sprouting horns

____

Task 3

Finish the following proverbs by choosing the animal words in the box.

lion	lamb	rabbit	fox	bat
fish	dog	peacock	wolf	swan
mouse	ox	chicken	horse	

1. As poor as a church ________________.
2. As timid as a ________________.
3. As blind as a ________________.
4. As strong as a ________________.
5. To drink like a ________________.
6. As cunning as a ________________.
7. As graceful as a ________________.
8. As proud as a ________________.
9. As tender as a ________________.
10. As greedy as a ________________.
11. As patient as an ________________.
12. As brave as a ________________.
13. As gentle as a ________________.
14. As faithful as a ________________.

4. Botanic Phrases

The long history and different traditions have endowed some plants with certain connotations that may vary across different cultures. In this section, you are going to learn, compare and practice different connotations of botanic phrases between Chinese and Western cultures.

Task 1

In Chinese and Western cultures, some botanic phrases have similar or even the same connotation, while others do not. So please classify the given animals into two catalogs by filling out the box below.

	laurel	thorn	cherry	willow
Botanic Phrases:	lotus	plum blossom	bamboo	pine
	rose	apple	oak	

Share Similar Connotation in Chinese and English	Have Different Connotations in Chinese and English

Task 2

Read the following sentences, translate them into Chinese. Pay particular attention to the connotations of the botanic phrases in each sentence.

1. Youngsters usually view the world with rose-colored eyes.

____

2. Preparing for the college entrance examination is no bed of roses.

____

3. An apple a day keeps the doctor away.

____

4. This conversation will end up nowhere as you are talking about apples and oranges.

____

5. This university owns the reputation of innovation. However, it has been resting on its laurel for a very long time.

____

6. The birthday party has been wonderful, and this exquisite gift is really a cherry on the cake.

____

7. She failed the exam, but the teacher decided to give her another bite at the cherry by allowing her to take the test again.

____

8. The young lady has been wearing the willow since her mother's funeral.

____

9. His father passed away three years ago and left him a good fortune. He has become a lotus eater ever since.

____

10. As the saying goes, there is no rose without a thorn. So nothing is perfect.

____

11. As an environmental activist when he was younger, my father was quite a thorn in the oil companies' sides at the time.

____

12. With a heart of oak, there is no obstacle you can't overcome.

____

5. Numbers

Number is a rather common element during intercultural communications, and even the most ordinary numbers may bear specific meanings if we take culture into account. During the translation or interpretation, the information gap on number may lead to misunderstandings or even conflicts. In this section, we are going to learn about numbers and their cultural implications.

Task 1

In writing decimals, most Europeans use commas (,) instead of decimal points (.) that are commonly used in China, American and other English-speaking cultures. Please complete the form based on existing numbers.

Countries	Number 1	Number 2	Number 3	Number 4
China				
Germany		8. 431		

to be continued

continued

Countries	Number 1	Number 2	Number 3	Number 4
France				34,5
UK	27.62			
USA			546, 345.5	

Task 2

In this task, you are going to look up the numbers listed in the tables and fill out the table with their meanings in different cultures.

Number	China	English-Speaking Countries
4		
13		
8		
5		

Task 3

In this task, you are going to read sentences with numbers. Please try to find out the meanings of numbers in these sentences and write them down on the lines below.

1. Tomorrow is a big day, I strongly recommend you to plan your day with a time table beforehand, or it will be at sixes and sevens.

sixes and sevens:

____

2. The third time is the charm.

Number three is always fortunate.

All good things go by threes.

three:

____

3. This second-hand watch was bought years ago from a sixpenny stall.

six:

4. A cat has nine lives.

A stitch in time saves nine.

nine:

5. If he truly belongs to the upper ten, why is he staying in this shabby room?

Stacy is a perfect ten. When Anthony met her at the first sight, he couldn't get her out of his mind.

ten:

6. The old lady was in the seventh heaven at meeting her long-lost son.

seven:

Section Ⅲ. Evaluation

Aspects of Learning Performance		Rating				
		1	2	3	4	5
1	I have deepened my understanding of escort interpretation in terms of cultural differences.					
2	I am able to translate English proverbs and idioms into Chinese and vice versa.					
3	I can tell the differences of color phrases in Chinese and English in terms of cultural connotation.					
4	I am able to use the color phrases correctly.					
5	I can tell the differences of animal phrases in Chinese and English in terms of cultural connotation.					
6	I am able to use the animal phrases correctly.					
7	I can tell the differences of botanic phrases in Chinese and English in terms of cultural connotation.					
8	I am able to use the botanic phrases correctly.					
9	I know about the cultural connotations of some numbers.					
10	I am able to translate numbers correctly.					
Remarks						

Section Ⅳ. Reflection and Summary

Unit 7　Travel and Making Friends

PPT

Section Ⅰ. Classification and Requirements

NO.	Aspects	Requirements	Others
1	Informal Communication	1. Can tell the factors that affect informal communication. 2. Be able to make informal communication including addressing people, greeting, initiating conversation, making invitation, parting, expressing gratitude and apology, making compliment, etc. in both Chinese and English.	
2	Travel Etiquette	Know about different travel etiquette in different countries.	
3	Different Friendships	1. Understand the different meanings of friendship in different cultures. 2. Know about the factors that may affect friendship.	
4	Foreign Food and Festivals	Know about some typical food and festivals in other cultures.	

Section Ⅱ. Classification of Travel and Making Friends

1. Informal Communication

1.1 Addressing People

Task 1

Can you recognize the following addressing terms? Do you know how to use them correctly? Can you use them to address Sara Philip Miller and Winston Lee Davis?

1. Sir 2. Madam 3. Miss 4. Mrs. 5. Mr. 6. Ms.

Task 2

Please write down some profession-respected titles in the box.

Example: teacher

Task 3

Please translate the following Chinese official titles into English.

1. 主席 ______________________
2. 书记 ______________________
3. 总理 ______________________
4. 部长 ______________________
5. 委员长 ______________________
6. 省长 ______________________
7. 副部长 ______________________
8. 副主席 ______________________
9. 副主任 ______________________

Task 4

Translate the following English academic titles into Chinese.

1. Professor ______

2. Associate professor ______

3. Academician ______

4. Research associate ______

5. Research associate of literature ______

6. (senior) research fellow (of…) ______

7. Associate research fellow (of…) ______

8. Assistant research fellow (of…) ______

1.2 Greeting

Task 1

Translate the following English greetings into Chinese and vice versa.

1. 久闻大名!

______

2. 幸会!

______

3. 好久不见!

______

4. How do you do?

______

5. How's going?

______

6. What's up?

______

Task 2

A Chinese staff ran into his English colleague on the street. They greeted each other:

Staff: Hello!

English colleague: Hi, how do you do?

Staff: Good, how are you getting on?

English colleague: (confused) I am fine, thank you!

1. Read the conversation above, discuss with your partner and try to explain why the English colleague was confused.

2. If you were the Chinese staff, what would you say to greet the English colleague?

Task 3

Read the following situations in which you are communicating with English-speaking people. Try to decide which answer is suitable in each situation. (You may choose more than one possible answer to each question.)

1. You are waiting in a hotel lobby next to a westerner, and you would like to start a conversation with him/her. Which of the following could you say to start the conversation?

A. Are you from America?

B. Are you expecting someone?

C. It's so hot outside today.

D. It's a beautiful hotel, isn't it?

2. You and your classmates are planning to visit your American teacher Jennifer Austin. In this case, what could you say to the teacher to arrange the visit?

A. Could you please inform us when you will be free? We are very much like to pay you a visit.

B. Ms. Austin, we want to visit you next week, please inform us a time that is convenient for you.

C. Ms. Austin, can we visit you next week? What time would be convenient for you?

D. Please tell us when you are free. We want to visit you.

3. One of your British friends has invited you to dinner, but you will be busy that evening and cannot accept the invitation. How would you respond?

A. I have something important to do that evening. Please suggest another time.

B. No. I will be busy that evening, so I have no time. Thank you.

C. I'd love to. But I'm afraid I will be busy that evening. Thank you all the same.

D. That would be lovely, but I'm afraid I have something to do on that evening. Would another evening be possible?

4. You have invited some westerners to dinner. Everybody is at the table, what would you say to start the meal?

A. Don't stand on ceremony. Let's eat.

B. This meal is very simple. Let's begin.

C. Do start.

D. Please help yourselves.

5. You run into your American teacher Jennifer Austin in a restaurant during the summer holiday. What could you say to greet her?

A. Hello, Ms. Austin, nice to meet you!

B. Hello, Ms. Austin, it's very nice meeting you!

C. Hello, Ms. Austin, lovely to see you here!

D. Hello, Ms. Austin, you must love the food here, don't you?

1.3 Initiating Conversations

Task 1

What conversational topics are acceptable to westerners? Circle them out.

family	hobbies	money	holidays	weather	age
salary	a local or national event		religion	health	
jobs	films	books	marital status		

Task 2

It's common knowledge to avoid talking about money or asking a westerner about how much they've paid for something. In this case, if you desperately wish to know the price, you may need to take a detour to get the answer. For example, if you want to know the price of your friend's new purse, how will you start the conversation? Write it down on the lines below.

____

____

1.4 Invitation

Task 1

Discuss the differences between Western and Chinese dinner invitation and fill out the table below.

Differences	In the West	In China
Invitation expectations	Both the husband and wife	
Declining an invitation	No detailed explanations	
Number of cuisines	Proper quantity	
Dining out habits	Share the cost of the meal equally among them, to go Dutch, or split the bill	

Task 2

Read the following two conversations. Which one is a genuine invitation, and why?

Conversation 1:

Ross: It's nice talking to you, but I have to take the bus now.

Julie: OK. Perhaps we can meet sometime later.

Ross: Sounds good. Why not drop in sometime?

Julie: Great. See you later.

Conversation 2:

Fred: I heard you are moving to Shanghai next month. Shall we have dinner together?

Linda: Sure. It's so nice of you. I'd love to.

Fred: What about 5 pm this Saturday at Lake Restaurant?

Linda: OK. See you then.

Task 3

Read the conversation between Frank (from America) and Ling (from China) and fulfill the tasks below.

Frank: It's so nice to talk to you. Maybe we can go to that museum together sometime.

Ling: I'd love to, but when?

Frank: What?

Ling: You said we could go to that museum together sometime, so when will that be?

Frank: Let's talk about it later, I have to go now. We can discuss on the phone.

Ling: Sure, I will be free this afternoon, can I call you then?

Frank: Of course, I am looking forward to hearing from you, but I will be so busy today.

Ling: How about tomorrow?

Frank: I'm not sure, we'll see. I really have to go now. See you later.

Ling: See you.

1. Discuss with your partner about Frank's invitation at the very beginning. Do you think it's a genuine invitation or a false one?

2. Analyze Ling's responses to Frank's invitation and find out the confusions or misunderstandings in the conversation.

3. If you were Ling, how will you respond to in the conversation? (You may refer to the different ways of declining in Western countries and China in Task 1.) Please rewrite the conversation below.

____

____

____

____

____

____

1.5 Parting

Task 1

Think about the common phrases for parting in Chinese and English, and fill out the table below.

Common Phrases for Parting in Chinese	Common Phrases for Parting in English

Task 2

You are about to leave after having a feast at one of your friends' home. What will you say to the host in Chinese and English ways? Please discuss in groups, fill out the table below, compare your answers with each other and explain the differences.

Chinese Way	English Way

1.6 Gratitude

Task 1

Read and compare the conversations and finish the tasks below.

(1) Identify and underline the inappropriate ways of appreciations and responses presented in the following conversations.

(2) Discuss in groups, try to explain the rationales under the differences between Chinese and English appreciations and responses.

Scenario:

Your colleague has just offered you a favor in the project, you are going to show your gratitude.

Conversation 1:

A: Thank you so much for what you have done for me, I'm really appreciate that.

B: You are very welcome.

Conversation 2:

A: Thank you, I am so sorry for all the troubles caused by me.

B: You don't need to apologize.

Conversation 3:

A: Thank you so much for what you have done for me, I'm really appreciate that.

B: You don't need to thank me!

A: (Why didn't he accept my appreciation?)

Task 2

Read the following expressions of gratitude. Rearrange them from the lowest degree of gratitude to the highest.

Common Expressions of Gratitude	Rearranged Order
Thank you very much. Thanks. I really don't know how to thank you enough. Thank you very much indeed. Many thanks.	

1.7 Apology

Read the following common expressions of apology. Rearrange them in order from formal to informal.

Common Expressions of Apology	Rearranged Order
Please forgive me (for…) I must beg to apologize for… I apologize. I'm terribly sorry for… May I offer you my sincerest apologies for… Excuse me. Sorry about that. I beg your pardon for…	

1.8 Compliment

Task 1

Compliments normally can be used to create or reinforce solidarity, to greet people, to express thanks or congratulations, to encourage, to soften criticism, to overcome embarrassment, or just to start a conversation. In this part, you are going to discuss and identify the function(s) of each compliment first and then write down your responses on the lines.

1. Professor Wang, is that your calligraphy? It's so beautiful, I like it so much!

Your response: ____________________

2. Good morning Jane, haven't seen you for a while. You look so good today! I like your new purse. It's so cute.

Your response: ____________________

3. What a beautiful dress! I like it so much. Thank you mother, it's the best present I have ever had.

Your response: ____________________

4. You guys have achieved a great progress in this season. Congratulations! I believe you can get a better ranking in the next season if you train harder in the next couple of months.

Your response: ____________________

5. Your article is clear and logical, it would be better if you have a better handwriting.

Your response: ____________________

6. I like your new hairstyle, which barber's do you go?

Your response: ____________________

7. It's just a story. Your heart is so pure and soft. Don't cry, we should be happy for them.

Your response: ____________________

Task 2

As a Chinese, do you think it's appropriate to praise the appearance of your friend's wife/husband? Why or why not? How would you reply to the compliment "your wife is really beautiful?" made by your American friend?

2. Travel Etiquette

Task 1

Read the following statements concerning travel etiquette in different countries. Decide true(T) or false(F).

(1) ____ In Brazil, women kiss each other in personal greetings, while men pat each other on the back.

(2) ____ In Brazil, people should put both hands above the table while dining.

(3) ____ In Canada, eating while walking on the street is a common sight.

(4) _____ Tipping is a common practice in Canada and USA.

(5) _____ In Germany, leaving a small amount of food on your plate is a way to show your politeness.

(6) _____ In Japan, you are expected to tip in a restaurant.

(7) _____ In Mexico, you should shake hands with each other when departing.

(8) _____ In Republic of Korea, a firm shake accompanied by eye contact is the usual way of greeting between men.

(9) _____ Fruit, flowers and candy are appropriate gifts when you are invited to a Korean home.

(10) _____ In USA, it is impolite to refuse the food offered by your host.

Task 2

Study in groups and answer the following questions.

(1) What are the differences of greetings between USA, Brazil, China and Japan?

(2) How do tipping customs vary in USA, Germany and Brazil?

(3) What are the cultural differences in dining practices between China, Japan and Republic of Korea?

(4) What are the cultural taboos concerning giving flowers as gifts in China, Canada and UK?

(5) Can you give some tips for traveling in Arabian countries?

3. Different Friendships

Task 1

The term "friendship" contains different meanings in different countries and cultures. It can be a strong life-long relationship between two people, or it can be ended when you move to another neighborhood. It can take decades to build a friendship in one culture but minutes in another. In this part, you are going to pick one foreign country as your research target, find out the meaning of friendship in the target country, fill out the form below and share your findings within groups.

Your Target Country	
How to Build a Friendship	
Friendship and Family life	

to be continued

continued

The Breakup of Friendship	

Task 2

Based on the above research, give some suggestions on how to make friends with people from your target country.

4. Foreign Food and Festivals

Task 1

Can you recognize the following foreign cuisines?

scone	cheese burger	lasagna
croissant	samosa	pizza
jacket potato	muffin	chicken tikka masala
fish and chips	pancake	pie
kebab	pasta	salad

Task 2

A pop quiz on western cuisines:

1. Pick out the most popular British food from the choices below.

   A. pizza B. mashed potatoes C. roast beef D. fish and chips

2. What is the most popular food for America's Thanksgiving?

   A. beef B. pork C. mutton D. turkey

3. Cheddar cheese is originally from which country?

   A. France B. America C. England D. Germany

4. Which of the following is not a kind of sauces?

   A. mayonnaise B. ketchup C. mustard D. fruit Loaf

5. Hot dogs and hamburgers are famous American food. However, both of them are based on traditional ________ food.

   A. English B. Chinese C. French D. German

Task 3

Pick a foreign cuisine that you are interested in, conduct a research on the cuisine and fill out the form below, and then introduce the cuisine to your classmates.

Name of the Cuisine	
What's the Origin Story of It?	
What's Special about It?	
Why Do You Choose It as Your Research Topic?	

Task 4

Since some festivals are unique carriers of cultural significance and historical evolution, celebrating festivals is a way to celebrate cultural and historical heritages. Please look at the following festivals, do you know the stories behind them? Try to match their countries of origin and their ways of celebration.

Festivals	Countries of Origin	Ways of Celebration
La Tomatina	USA	It often lasts for three days. During these days, revelers are expected to get drenched with water. Although its initial purpose is to wash away bad luck and get purified, this festival is now morphed into a joyous occasion.
Diwali	Thailand	It is known as the largest beer festival in the world and launched in September every year. The drinking often takes place in beer tents run by the breweries, and one needs to have a seat in order to get a drink. In addition to beer, there are also some other traditional foods such as pretzels, dumplings and cheese noodles for consumption.
Burning Man	Germany	It is the largest food fight in the world. Tons of ripe tomatoes are dumped on to the ground and people throw them at each other for almost an hour when everyone is covered with red juice.
Songkran	India	This festival is celebrated in Black Rock Desert, Nevada. People dress in highly personal gear, and are free to create artworks, sculptures, vehicles or just cycle around the desert to greet fellow travelers during the one-week festival. On the last evening, a giant wooden effigy which symbolizes summer would be burned.
Oktoberfeast	Spain	It's the festival to celebrate the victory of good over evil, light over darkness. Traditionally, every household lights their lamps. People also clean their houses to welcome Lakshimi, the goddess of wealth and prosperity.

Task 5

How much do you know about the following festivals? Pick a festival that interests you, conduct a research and introduce the festival to your classmates.

Rio Carnival (Brazil)	Sun Festival (Egypt)
Ice&Snow Festival (China)	Gion Matsuri (Japan)
Moomba Festival (Australia)	Il Palio (Italy)

Section Ⅲ. Evaluation

Aspects of Learning Performance		Rating				
		1	2	3	4	5
1	I have deepened my understanding of travel abroad and making foreign friends.					
2	I can tell some factors that affect communication in other cultures.					
3	I am able to make informal communication in both Chinese and English.					
4	I can tell the differences between Chinese and English in terms of informal communication such as greeting, parting, expressing gratitude, etc.					
5	I know different travel etiquette in different cultures.					
6	I can tell the different meanings of friendship in different cultures.					
7	I know the factors that may affect friendship.					
8	I will take cultural factors into consideration when building friendships with people from another culture.					
9	I can tell some typical food in other cultures.					
10	I know some common festivals in other countries.					
Remarks						

Section Ⅳ. Reflection and Summary

Reference

[1] 毕继万. 跨文化非语言交际 [M]. 北京：外语教学与研究出版社，1998.

[2] 房玉靖. 跨文化交际实训 [M]. 北京：对外经济贸易大学出版社，2014.

[3] 何明霞. 国际商业文化简明教程 [M]. 2 版. 上海：上海外语教育出版社，2018.

[4] 胡文仲. 跨文化交际学概论 [M]. 北京：外语教学与研究出版社，1999.

[5] 黄育才. 跨文化交际实用英语教程 [M]. 2 版. 上海：复旦大学出版社，2019.

[6] 金惠康. 跨文化交际翻译 [M]. 北京：中国对外出版集团，2003.

[7] 莫爱屏. 跨文化交际教程 [M]. 北京：北京大学出版社，2016.

[8] 许力生. 新编跨文化交际英语教程 [M]. 上海：上海外语教育出版社，2013.

[9] 余卫华. 跨文化交际教程 [M]. 杭州：浙江大学出版社，2019.

[10] 余卫华. 跨文化交际原理与应用 [M]. 北京：清华大学出版社，2022.

[11] 朱建新. 跨文化交际与礼仪 [M]. 南京：东南大学出版社，2019.

[12] 郑晓泉. 跨文化交际 [M]. 杭州：浙江大学出版社，2021.

[13] Lillian H. Chaney, Jeanette S. Martin. Intercultural business communication [M]. 6th ed. London: Pearson Education Limited, 2014.